$125

DATE DUE

N

DEMCO INC 38-2971

Keyboard Instruments

IN THE METROPOLITAN MUSEUM OF ART

A Picture Book

by Emanuel Winternitz

CURATOR OF MUSICAL INSTRUMENTS

THE METROPOLITAN MUSEUM
OF ART, NEW YORK 1961

FRONTISPIECE: Harpsichord.

Italian, late XVII century.
Anonymous Gift, 1945

Introduction

Riccho son doro · et, riccho son di svono,
Non mi sonar si tv non ha del bvono.

"Rich am I in gold and rich am I in tone:
If thy music be not noble, then leave my keys alone."

Inscription on a spinettino made for Eleonora d'Este

AMONG THE most complex and intriguing of all artifacts are musical instruments, for they please both eye and ear. They are technical contrivances for producing sound and are subject to the stern laws of physics and acoustics as well as to the ever-changing phases in the evolution of musical thought. As decorative objects, often designed as furniture, they also reflect the changes in visual taste throughout history. This is one of the reasons why collections of musical instruments find their logical place among the various objects, many of them also tools, in an art museum devoted to the systematic interpretation of past cultures through the display of their artifacts. Musical instruments represent one of the many threads in that dense contrapuntal fabric called civilization.

The Middle Ages conceived of music as one of the noble sisters of the quadrivium, together with what today we consider sciences: arithmetic, geometry, and astronomy. Later a gradual transformation took place, and Pollaiuolo's pairing of an allegory of music with one of linear perspective on the tomb of Pope Sixtus IV is symptomatic of the new role of music as one of the "creative" arts. It is significant that in the *trompe-l'oeil* intarsias of the quattrocento study of Federigo da Montefeltro from his palace in Gubbio (now in the Metropolitan Museum) musical instruments play a predominant role among the many tools of the arts and sciences of his time. The fifteenth century also witnessed the growth of the first systematic collections of musical instruments. In the sixteenth, the intertwining of music and the visual arts was reflected in special collections of musical instruments that were prized not only as specimens of ingenious craftsmanship but also as objects of refined beauty. These instrument museums were distinct from the *Musikkammern*, in which were kept the instruments regularly needed for actual performance; the museums comprehended those regarded as rarities, antiquities, or mechanical curiosities and those treasured simply as showpieces. They were housed in many famous *grotti, camerini,* and *stanzini* along with paintings, statues, and other works of art. Venice, in particular, was famous for its unique collections of musical instruments: Francesco Sansovino in his *Venezia descritta* (1581) devotes a special chapter to the *studi di musica* in that city. Other rich musical collections were those of the Fuggers of Augsburg, of Alfonso II of Ferrara, of Archduke Karl of Styria in Graz, and of the Florentine sculptor Ridolfo Sirigatti. Later, in the baroque period, Rome excelled in this field. Two Jesuits, both deeply interested in the history of musical instruments, Athanasius Kircher in his *Musurgia* (1650) and F. Filippo Bonnani in his *Gabinetto armonico* (1722), mention the Galleria Armonica belonging to Michele Todini, abounding in the complex musical machines and automata so fashionable at that time. Among the pieces in this museum was the gilded harpsichord borne by tritons and mermaids, now in the Metropolitan Museum, to be discussed later.

The Crosby Brown Collection of Musical Instruments of All Nations in the Metropolitan Museum, the earliest and by far the largest collection of musical instruments in this hemisphere, has a history of nearly one hundred years. In the 1870s in Florence, Mrs. John Crosby Brown fell in love with a little ivory lute and bought it. Thus began a lifelong infatuation that resulted, thirty years later, in one of the richest collections of musical instruments in the world, systematically selected to represent the various cultural orbits as well as the gradual evolution of instrumental types. The catalogue, pub-lished between 1903 and 1914, comprises six volumes, covering Europe, Asia, Africa, America and Oceania, Historical Groups, and Keyboard Instruments. In recent years the collection has been enriched by further donations and purchases and contains today nearly four thousand instruments.

Our extensive collection of keyboard instruments in particular has contributed to the modern revival of interest in these instruments: by providing models for the manufacture of reconstructions and replicas, it has served as a stimulus for the recent trend toward "authentic" performances. There is hardly any need to stress the ever-growing educational importance of a collection such as this. Our eclectic age, perhaps more history-conscious than any before, is most curious to reconstruct the sound of the music of earlier centuries. Scholars, students, and practical musicians turn to our instruments to find out what the timbre and the technical potentialities of instruments were in the time of William Byrd, Orlando Gibbons, or Domenico Scarlatti or how Mozart's and Beethoven's pianos differed from ours in tone, compass, and touch.

The Museum's collection contains a long line of keyboard instruments from the Renaissance to modern times, including clavichords, harpsichords, pianos, organs, and a considerable number of types that are less common today than in the past, such as harmoniums, glassichords, glockenspiels, and orphicas. This booklet illustrates those examples that reflect most characteristically the successive stages in the evolution of the keyboard and that best reveal the dual role of the musical instrument as tool of music and work of art.

A viola da braccio, hurdy-gurdy, trumpet, horn, reed pipe, and Panpipe.
Detail of the intarsia decoration on the lid of 26

Evolution of the Keyboard

1. Monochord. Woodcut from Lodovico Fogliano's Musica theorica (1529)

In the push-button society we live in today, the keyboard, be it on a typewriter, an IBM machine, or a piano, has become such an indispensable part of our mechanized world that it is taken for granted. However, for the historian and student of music, it may not be without interest to examine the nature and origin of this significant development in musical history. One may define a keyboard as a set of levers that serve as an extension of the player's fingers: when he depresses them they enable him to control distant points in the mechanism of his instrument. So simple is the keyboard in principle that one cannot but wonder why it was not invented by ancient peoples with highly developed technology, such as the Egyptians, the Greeks, and the Romans. Aristotle mentions cogwheel mechanisms, the Egyptians of Ptolemaic times pumped water by machinery, and Vitruvius describes mechanical gadgets to measure the mileage of the horse-drawn Roman "taxis" and, in the field of music, an elaborate hydraulic organ. Why then was the keyboard not invented until the Middle Ages?

Perhaps the answer lies in the interaction between musical thought and the tools of music; the realm of matter functions, as it were, as a floodgate for the stream of ideas. The structure of ancient Greek music, Gregorian and Byzantine chant, and, later still, the music of the twelfth century troubadours and trouvères was predominantly monophonic: it consisted of a single melodic line with no accompaniment or only a simple one. As long as this musical structure prevailed, there was no need for a mechanism that could produce several simultaneous voices—in other words, polyphony. Only after the rise of polyphony in the Occident could people conceive of an instrument that would bring into the reach of one player the voices or melodic strands produced by several singers or players. Only after the final victory of this style were keyboards in their modern sense—that is, with rapid control of numerous simultaneous tones—constructed.

The origin of the modern keyboard dates back to the Middle Ages. Among its antecedents are the levers used in the monochord, the organistrum, and the early pipe organ. Medieval monks used the monochord to determine the precise dependence of the musical intervals upon certain arithmetical ratios of length of string. It was an oblong wooden box with one string, later several, stretched over its sounding board. The strings were stopped by movable bridges that had to be raised or lowered by the player's hands. Eventually these bridges were replaced by more practical and rapidly responding levers so pivoted that when the front of the lever was depressed by the player's finger, the rear part was raised toward the string. Though there are no treatises to substantiate this, it would seem logical to assume that this early key mechanism played an important role in the development of the clavichord, which as late as the Renaissance was still called *monocordium* or *manicordo*. The fifteenth century clavichord that is depicted in the intarsias of another study of Federigo da Montefeltro, this time in his palace at Urbino, is so large and complex that it must be considered the fruit of an already lengthy evolution.

Another and more primitive key mechanism is found in the medieval organistrum, frequently represented among the instruments played by the twenty-four Apocalyptical Elders in the tympana

2. *Wheel and stopping mechanism of a French* XVIII *century hurdy-gurdy*

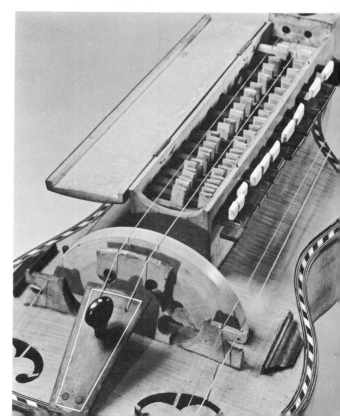

of Romanesque churches, as at Moissac and Santiago de Compostela. Its strings, stretched over a long, rectangular soundbox, were vibrated by a wheel turned by a crank at the end of the instrument. One player turned the crank while the other manipulated with both hands a set of stopping rods that raised small bridges placed beneath the strings. The handles of the rods were on the upper side of the instrument as it lay across the laps of both players, and therefore the rods could not fall away from the strings of their own weight. The organistrum was the ancestor of the hurdy-gurdy (vielle à roue or "fiddle with a wheel"), which is still played by French peasants. Just when it was improved we do not know, but in frescoes of the school of Giotto the modern hurdy-gurdy keyboard is clearly shown. The stopping rods are now on the lower side and thus fall back automatically; a single player can push them with one hand while turning the crank with the other.

The pipe organ acquired a keyboard relatively late. Giant instruments like the tenth century organ in the monastery at Winchester, with no less than four hundred pipes and twenty-six bellows pumped by seventy men, had no keyboards in the modern sense, but rather a row of slides called *linguae*, or "tongues." These were wooden boards that projected from the wind chest and could be pulled out to open the channels leading from the wind chest to all the pipes of the same pitch. They were cumbersome and ran in wooden grooves. One can imagine what the damp English climate did to them—and also what muscle power was demanded of the player, who could not have manipulated them in rapid succession. No wonder a smoother method of operation was sought. The solution was

found in the eleventh century when the tongues were replaced by wooden levers that could be depressed vertically to open valves inside the wind chest and allow the compressed air to flow into the pipes. Clumsy as these primitive keys must have been, they were an important step in the gradual evolution of the keyboard that, after many centuries of development, culminated in the keys of the modern organ, which at the lightest touch instantaneously release the sound of many hundreds of pipes. An early landmark in this evolution was the organ in the cathedral of Magdeburg at the end of the eleventh century: it had a fully developed keyboard of sixteen notes. Early keyboards were sometimes inside the wind chest and therefore not visible in many representations found in paintings and sculpture. What we often see are push-buttons similar to those of a modern accordion; when they were pushed they depressed the front ends of the hidden keys.

It is not until the Renaissance that one finds the question of the origin of the keyboard posed in musical treatises, with answers based rather on guesswork than on historical evidence. Vincenzo Galilei, the father of the famous astronomer, wrote an ingenious book, *Dialogo della musica antica e della moderna* (Florence, 1581), in which he relates the invention of the harpsichord—which he does not call by the later Italian term *clavicembalum* ("cymbalum with keys"), but rather *harpicordo*— to the harp. "Although Italian musicians claim it as their invention, it had its origin in the harp, and is really nothing but a horizontal harp with keys added," he says, pointing as proof to the similarity in name and shape and in the number, disposition, and material of the strings.

Clavichords
and Harpsichords

OF ALL THE keyboard instruments, the clavichord is the simplest in construction and probably the oldest. When the finger depresses the key, a little brass plate called the tangent, attached to the rear part of the key, not only strikes the string to make it vibrate, but also divides it into two parts, one of which is deadened by a damping cloth. In the earlier, "fretted" clavichord, one string could be struck at different times by more than one tangent, thereby producing more than one tone. It was not until the eighteenth century that the fretted clavichord was gradually replaced by the unfretted type, which had a different string for each key. Though the tone of the clavichord is extremely soft, the volume can be modified by finger pressure, an effect not possible at the harpsichord.

3. Fretted clavichord. German, first half of the XVIII century. The Crosby Brown Collection, 1889

The Museum has examples of both types, among them an eighteenth century fretted clavichord (3) with a compass of four octaves, and a large unfretted one (4) of Karl Philipp Emanuel Bach's time, made by John Christopher Jesse in Halberstadt.

In instruments of the harpsichord family the strings are plucked by quills or leather plectra, which disengage immediately after contact with the string. Thus tone volume cannot be modified by finger pressure but only by adding more strings— that is, by bringing one or more sets of strings into play by means of the stops. The Museum's collec-

4. *Unfretted clavichord, by John Christopher Jesse. German (Halberstadt), 1765. The Crosby Brown Collection, 1889*

5. *Spinettino. Italian (Venice), 1540. Inscribed: "Ordinata e fatta per Sua Eccelenza la Sigra Duchesa D'Urbino L'Anno di Nostra Salute 1540 e pagata 250 Scudi Romani." Purchase, 1953, Joseph Pulitzer Bequest*

tion has instruments of many shapes and sizes: rectangular Flemish virginals with strings running from left to right, Italian clavicembali of "grand" shape with strings running front to rear, and pentagonal and other polygonal spinets and spinettini.

A little spinettino (5) that was made in 1540 in Venice for Eleonora d'Este, duchess of Urbino, is a recent addition to the Museum's collection, and although it is one of the oldest keyboard instruments we have, it is still in perfect playing condition. Devotion to fine musical instruments was a tradition in the Este family, and Eleonora's mother, Isabella d'Este, who was an expert clavichord player herself, kept jealous count of the precious instruments possessed by her sister at the Sforza court in Milan, with an eye to securing them at her sister's death. This spinettino is profusely but unostentatiously decorated with a subtle combination of carving, intarsia, and certosino work. Even the jack rail and the buttons are made of layers of various woods, and its sunken sound-hole rose is of particular beauty. Back of the small strip of wood bearing the inscription mentioned earlier is written, in Italian chancery of the sixteenth century, the price of the instrument and its commission by Eleonora d'Este.

Among the most interesting Flemish instruments in existence is the double virginal (6) built by Hans Ruckers the Elder in Antwerp in 1581. Ruckers was the founder of the most famous Flemish dynasty of harpsichord makers and was admitted as *Claversinbalmakerre* to the Guild of Saint Luke in 1579. Ours is the oldest double virginal in existence: it consists actually of two instruments, each with its own

Sunken sound-hole rose of 5

Detail of the inlay and certosino work of 5

NAR SI TV NON HA DEL BVONO.

[13]

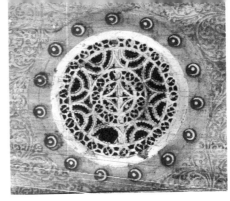

Metal sound-hole rose of 6

6. Double virginal, by Hans Ruckers the Elder.
Flemish (Antwerp), 1581. Gift of B. H. Homan, 1929

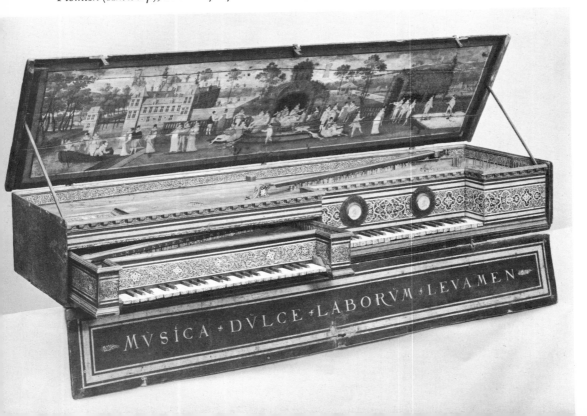

MVSICA · DVLCE · LABORVM · LEVAMEN

Initials of Hans Ruckers on the lid of the small box at the left of the soundboard of 6. The box held a tuning key and extra quills and strings

A musical party. Detail of the painting inside the lid of 6

7. Double virginal, by Lodewijck Grauwels.
Flemish, 1600. The Crosby Brown
Collection, 1889

Sound-hole rose of 7, showing Pan playing
a gigantic Panpipe, flanked by the
maker's initials

strings, jacks, and keys. The smaller one (*ottavino*) was inserted, like a drawer, under the soundboard of the larger instrument and was shorter in compass, higher in pitch, and lighter in tone and timbre. It could be removed for traveling.

Lodewijck Grauwels or, as he signed his instruments, Ludovicus Grovvelus continued the tradition of Hans Ruckers. The beautiful double virginal he made in 1600 (7) is the only one by this craftsman known to have survived. The original *ottavino*, which was lost, has been replaced by Arnold Dolmetsch, the well-known English connoisseur and builder of replicas of old instruments.

Because of their size and flat surfaces, harpsichords and organs lent themselves particularly well to pictorial decoration, which in fact continued the fifteenth century tradition of the painted *cassoni*. They also offered unlimited opportunities for intarsia, certosino work, and carving, as for instance the many elaborate sound holes made of wood, parchment, or metal.

Different decorative traditions developed in the north and south. Flemish virginals, whose oblong coffinlike cases were usually painted black and devoid of any exterior embellishment, were lavishly decorated inside. Their soundboards were adorned with painted flowers and pewter sound-hole roses, the insides of the upper lids with landscapes or Biblical or mythological subjects, the front covers with Latin proverbs, and large sections of the cases with wallpaper patterns. Italian harpsichords, on the other hand, were constructed in two parts: the instrument itself and a protective outer case from which it could be removed. This outer case was usually built by a different cabinetmaker from the

Putto riding on a sea shell borne by dolphins. Detail of 8

Triton, one of the three supporting the body of 8

one who had made the instrument and was apt to be more profusely decorated, often being covered with painting or stucco. The soundboard was left unpainted, its sole adornment a geometrical rose, frequently sunken—a true miniature architecture.

Most of the subjects painted inside the lids of harpsichords were related to music: Apollo, Amphion, Arion, Sappho, Parnassus, the Muses, King David, Saint Cecilia, angel concerts, and so forth. An exquisite painting by Bronzino of one of the most typical subjects, the contest between Apollo and Marsyas, is now in the Hermitage Museum in Leningrad. Its unusual form, originally wing-shaped but later expanded into a rectangle, indicates that it was intended for the decoration of a harpsichord lid.

[18]

8. Harpsichord. Italian (Rome), XVII *century. The Crosby Brown Collection, 1889*

Polyphemus playing a bagpipe.
One of the two figures flanking 8

The most elaborate instructions written during the High Renaissance for the pictorial decoration of keyboard instruments are to be found in the *Trattato dell' arte della pittura, scultura ed architettura* (1584) by Giovanni Paolo Lomazzo. For the ornamentation of church organs he recommends a long list of sacred topics, all of which should have some inner relation to music, thus ruling out such portrayals as the conversion of Saint Paul, the Annunciation, battle scenes, sacrifices, and miracles. The secular instruments, those used at court and in private homes, were to be decorated with mythological or allegorical subjects or representations of the nine choirs of heavenly musicians. Each choir should be devoted to one type of instrument and should contain portraits of the three most excellent musicians associated with it. He suggests twenty-seven famous musicians, among them Leonardo da Vinci, who was renowned for his virtuosity on the lira da braccio.

One outstanding example of baroque decorative art is the gilded harpsichord (8) of fantastic shape in the Museum's collection. Its wing-shaped body is supported by three fishtailed tritons and surrounded by sea nymphs and a putto perched on a sea shell, driving two dolphins—a veritable oceanic phantasmagoria. One side is decorated with an elaborate gilded frieze representing the triumph of Galatea, and the entire harpsichord is flanked by two life-size figures, each sitting on a rock: one represents Polyphemus playing a bagpipe and the other evidently Galatea, who must once have held a lute. The origins of this unusual instrument were unknown until shortly after the last war, when, quite by chance, I found in the storerooms of the

9. *Clavicytherium (clavicembalo verticale).*
Italian, early XVII *century. Two sets of unison*
strings; leather plectra.
The Crosby Brown Collection, 1889

10. Harpsichord, by Joannes Couchet. Flemish, about 1650. Two manuals; three sets of strings (one octave, two unison) and a lute stop. The Crosby Brown Collection, 1889

Palazzo Venezia in Rome a box of small and broken clay fragments, one of which strangely resembled the head of our Polyphemus. When reassembled the fragments turned out to be the little model for the gilded harpsichord, probably made by no lesser hand than that of Algardi. A second stroke of luck led to the discovery that the instrument had been part of Michele Todini's Galleria Armonica (founded before 1676) and was described in detail in a special chapter of Todini's catalogue, *Descrittione della machina di Polifemo e Galatea.*

Very early in the history of the harpsichord, instruments called clavicytheria were built with vertical soundboards. An illustration of one occurs as early as in the amusing dialogue on musical instruments, *Musica getutscht,* written by the German priest Sebastian Virdung in 1511. The Museum has a seventeenth century Italian clavicytherium (9) which is remarkable for its decoration. Both outside and inside the folding doors are painted angels playing musical instruments, and the area left by the curving outline of the trapezoidal soundboard is decorated with a painting of King David playing the harp, which snuggles cozily into the concave curvature of the soundboard.

A new era of harpsichord building was initiated by Joannes Couchet, nephew and successor of Hans Ruckers, who created the first instrument ideally suited to the keyboard music of the baroque. He transformed the typical Renaissance harpsichord into an instrument that permitted the two

Detail of 10 showing the four rows of jacks and the four buttons that operate the stops

Detail of the manuals of 10

[23]

manuals to be used simultaneously, thus greatly expanding the number of possible combinations of volume and tone color. A splendid example of his workmanship (10), with two manuals and four stops, is in the Museum's collection. His instruments were popular both with amateurs and professional musicians, and among his patrons were the two Chambonnières, famous French virtuoso-composers of the period.

Italian clavicembali were, as a rule, relatively simple in construction. They usually had one keyboard and two sets of eight-foot ("unison") strings, which provided only two levels of tone volume and

Carved wooden sound-hole rose of 12

*11. Spinet, by Charles Haward.
English, 1684. Leather plectra.
Gift of Joseph W. Drexel, 1889*

12. Harpsichord, by Girolamo Zenti.
Italian (Rome), 1658. Two sets of
unison strings; quill plectra.
Funds from Various Donors, 1886

Carved wooden sound-hole rose of 13

13. Harpsichord, by Girolamo Zenti. Italian (Rome), 1666. Two sets of unison strings; leather plectra. The Crosby Brown Collection, 1889

no gradation in timbre. Of this general type are two beautiful harpsichords by Girolamo Zenti (Hieronymus de Zentis) of Viterbo, who worked first in Rome and was later appointed harpsichord maker to Charles II of England. Both these instruments date from his Roman period (1658 and 1666), but they are quite different in size and decoration. The early one (12) is the smaller, and its exterior case is painted with cupids and wreaths of flowers; inside the lid is a pastoral scene, and the soundboard has a sunken rose of exceptional beauty. The decoration of the later instrument (13) is of a more purely ornamental nature, and its rich and full-bodied tone suggests that it was used as a continuo instrument in church or theater.

A late seventeenth century Italian harpsichord (Frontispiece), recently donated to the Museum, has a more complex arrangement—three sets of unison strings (one possibly producing a different timbre or tuned at a higher pitch), all operated by one manual. The instrument is exquisitely decorated. The body rests on three gilded columns, between two of which a mermaid is sitting—most likely the device of the Colonna family. The landscapes inside the cover strongly suggest the school of Gaspard Dughet (the brother-in-law of Poussin), who painted similar ones in the Palazzo Doria in Rome.

The variety of stops and the necessity of changing them during playing forced the musician, as late as and even later than Bach's time, to take one hand off the harpsichord keys in order to work the levers controlling the stops. (Pedals for harpsichords are an invention of twentieth century makers.) As early as the eighteenth century an attempt was made to circumvent this difficulty by the combina-

14. Harpsichord, by Vincenzo Sodi. Italian (Florence), 1779. Three manuals; no stops.
The Crosby Brown Collection, 1889

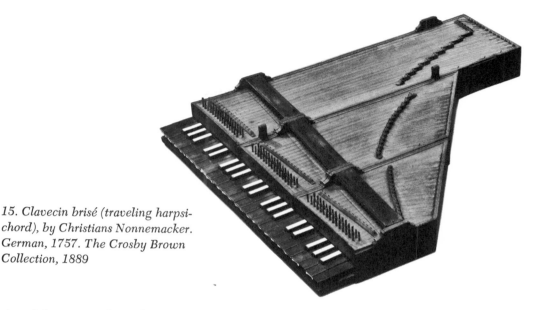

15. *Clavecin brisé (traveling harpsichord), by Christians Nonnemacker. German, 1757. The Crosby Brown Collection, 1889*

tion of three manuals, each of them corresponding to a different stop and thereby eliminating the awkward lever mechanism. Very few of these three-manual instruments are in existence, and one of them, made by Vincenzo Sodi in 1779 in Florence (14), is in the Museum's collection. The top keyboard acts on the octave strings, the middle on one unison and the octave, and the lower keyboard on the two sets of unison strings.

Some instruments owe their survival to surgical alteration. Harpsichords were often too expensive and too beautiful as furniture to be thrown away when the piano conquered the scene, and many of them were transformed into pianos. The large instrument made by Joannes Goermans in Paris in 1754 (16) had two manuals operating one four-foot stop and two eight-foot stops. One keyboard was later removed and replaced by a simple hammer action. The decoration is of great distinction. The soundboard, in typical Flemish style, is painted with flowers and birds, its pewter rose showing an angel playing a harp flanked by the maker's initials, while the *chinoiserie* on the lid and walls of the case includes groups of musicians with recorders, viols, a musette, and a two-manual harpsichord.

Even while traveling, connoisseurs did not like to be without music—hence the fashion for the clavecin brisé or clavecin de voyage. In the Museum's example (15) the soundboard consists of three sections hinged together, and they form a handy oblong box when folded on top of each other. Frederick the Great allegedly kept one of these instruments with him at all times during his military campaigns.

16. Harpsichord, by Joannes Goermans. French (Paris), 1754. This instrument, originally with two keyboards, was later rebuilt into a pianoforte. Anonymous Gift, 1944

Details of the chinoiserie inside the lid of 16. Above, musicians playing a two-manual harpsichord, a recorder, and fantastic fiddles. Below, a musette player. The score is of a "cotillon," a XVII century French dance

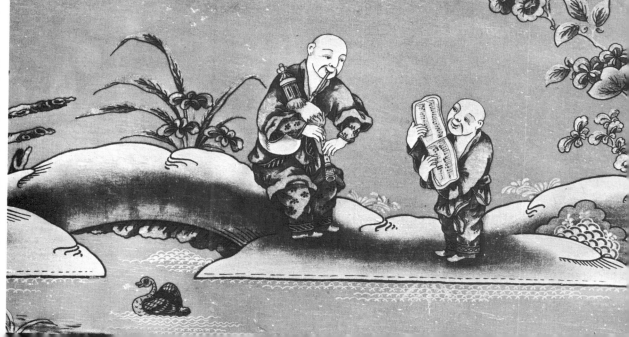

17. Cabinet organ. German, early XVII century. One set of metal pipes arranged in two rows. The Crosby Brown Collection, 1889

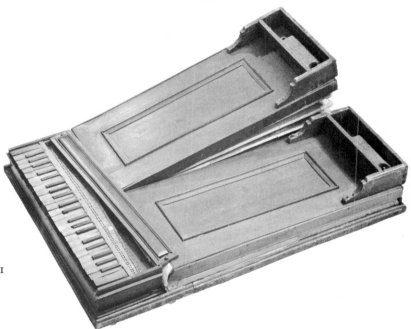

18. Regal. German, XVII *or* XVIII *century. The Crosby Brown Collection, 1889*

THE FOURTEENTH and fifteenth centuries brought great improvements in organ building, as the instrument was gradually adapted to Gothic polyphony. Many large churches had two organs: a big one in the nave—or later, over the main portal —for solo performances, and a smaller one in the choir for accompanying singers and for playing during the daily service.

Apart from the large church organs which developed during the Renaissance and the baroque period, several smaller types—chamber organs, positive organs, portative organs, and regals—evolved. All these are represented in the Museum's collection, but I will mention only a seventeenth century German cabinet organ (17) decorated with paintings, carved figures, and ivory plaques, and a large Bavarian or Austrian chamber organ (19) with four sets of pipes, dated 1758, with a painting on its front by Franz Casppar Hofer showing Saint Cecilia playing the organ accompanied by an angel playing a bass viola da gamba, in a super-baroque architectural setting.

The Museum also has several regals, portable organs with small metal pipes whose brass reeds produce the instrument's characteristic nasal, bleating tone; one of them, a large seventeenth or eighteenth century regal (18), has frequently been used in the Museum's concerts of early music.

19. Chamber organ.
South German, 1758.
The Crosby Brown Collection, 1889

The wooden and metal pipes of 19.
The pipes seen on the front of the
instrument are false

Saint Cecilia playing the organ. Detail of 19

Pianofortes

THE IDEA of a keyboard instrument with a hammer mechanism was in the air in the early eighteenth century. Musicians wanted an instrument whose loudness of sound could be controlled by finger pressure, and which would not be restricted to the terrace dynamics of the harpsichord and the organ, neither of which could switch from one dynamic level to another without a change of gears, as it were, when stops were pulled to bring fewer or more sets of strings or pipes into play. Bartolommeo Cristofori, curator of the collection of musical instruments at the Medici court, invented the gravicembalo con piano e forte, or in today's terminology the pianoforte, and in 1720 he built the instrument now in the Museum's collection (20). Only two of Cristofori's pianos have survived and ours is the elder. *Gravicembalo* is actually a variant of *clavicembalo,* meaning harpsichord. Cristofori's pianoforte, in fact, still resembled the harpsichord in many respects: shape, soundboard, keyboard, and strings. The jack and quill action of the harpsichord was, however, replaced by a hammer mechanism. The harpsichord jacks remained, but they were used only for carrying the felts of the dampers. The action is a miracle of precision and efficiency. That it includes an escapement, the device that lets the hammer fall back immediately after striking the string and thereby allows faster playing, attests to Cristofori's genius.

It was only after the middle of the eighteenth century that important composers began to write specifically for the pianoforte, exploiting its expressive capacity and great range of dynamic shadings. More than any composer of his time, Karl Philipp Emanuel Bach, Johann Sebastian's second son, was responsible for the development of the new "pianistic" style; his influence is clear in the piano works of Haydn and the young Beethoven. The triumph of the pianoforte over the harpsichord coincided with the rise to international fame of virtuosos like Mozart and Clementi. Clementi's first piano sonata, composed in 1773, is entirely adapted to the new medium. Mozart's twenty-six piano concertos were written between 1773 and 1791, and Beethoven's first in 1795. But for many years music dealers continued to sell scores of keyboard music, through the first eight of Beethoven's sonatas, indiscriminately *pour le clavecin ou pianoforte.*

Piano manufacturers, at first mainly in southern Germany and in England, began to compete to develop action, dynamics, and tone. The most outstanding German builder, and certainly the most influential historically, was Johann Andreas Stein of Augsburg. He had been apprentice to Gottfried

20. *Pianoforte, by Bartolommeo Cristofori. Italian (Florence), 1720. Inscribed: "Bartholomaeus de Christophoris Patavinus Inventor Faciebat Florentiae, MDCCXX."*
The Crosby Brown Collection, 1889

Silbermann, the great organ and piano builder for Frederick the Great and close friend of Johann Sebastian Bach (who nevertheless had strong reservations about his pianos). Stein's pianos were unsurpassed in lightness of touch and in quick response, and became Mozart's favorite instruments. The Museum's Stein piano (21) is of particular interest for it seems to be the only surviving pianoforte built by this maker with a pedal keyboard. The pedal keys are connected to a set of levers—similar to the tracker mechanism of an organ—which activate hammers that strike the bass strings. The harpsichord with a pedal keyboard was not unusual as a home practicing instrument for organists; and, although its piano counterpart was never widespread, still special music was written for the latter as late as Schumann's Opus 56 and Opus 58.

In London the outstanding piano makers were German and Swiss immigrants: Johann Zumpe, Burkhardt Tschudi, and the latter's son-in-law and partner John Broadwood. We have instruments by each of them, some of "grand" shape (see 23) with strings running from the front to the rear of the instrument, and others of square shape (see 22) with strings running from left to right parallel to the keyboard. The development of the piano was so rapid that Beethoven's later works, beginning with the Waldstein Sonata (Opus 53) in 1804,

Demonstration model of Cristofori hammer action

*Back view of the two levels of the Cristofori action.
Lower section, keys with catches and pushes;
upper section, hammers*

would not have been thinkable on Mozart's lighter and smaller instruments.

The first American pianos were built in Philadelphia and Boston in the 1770s, along English lines. The United States contributed significantly to the development of the modern piano through two inventions made in the 1820s by the Boston firm of A. Babcock: cross-stringing, an arrangement of strings in two levels which increased sonority, and the cast-iron frame, made possible by the progress of English and American iron production. The latter invention permitted heavier strings that, in addition to further increasing sonority, allowed a fuller dynamic range and gave the instrument greater resistance to the caprices of climate.

Early in the nineteenth century the piano became an article of mass production. Competing manufacturers advertised in the press and at international exhibitions and demonstrated their instruments in their own *salons de concert,* many of which—notably those of Erard and Pleyel in Paris and Bösendorfer in Vienna—became centers of musical life. The peak of the piano's prestige was reached with the works of Chopin, who confined his creative energies solely to that instrument, and with the world-wide fame of the virtuoso Liszt. About the same time, the piano became an indispensable part of the middle-class household, and

Detail of the keys and hammers of 20

*Back view of 21. The levers connect
the pedal keyboard to hammers
striking the bass strings*

Maker's label on the soundboard of 21

*Detail of 21 showing keys and wrest
plank with tuning pins and bridge*

21. Pianoforte with pedal attachment (Pedalflügel), by Johann Andreas Stein. Bavarian (Augsburg), 1778. The Crosby Brown Collection, 1889

22. Pianoforte, by Johann Zumpe.
English (London), 1767. The Crosby
Brown Collection, 1889

23. Pianoforte, by John
Broadwood. English
(London), 1792. English
grand action; three strings
to each key and two pedals,
one operating una corda,
the other lifting the dampers.
Gift of Mr. and Mrs.
Jerome C. Neuhoff, 1957

Detail of 23

24. *Pianoforte, by Loud Brothers. American (Philadelphia), early* XIX *century.*
The Crosby Brown Collection, 1889

no museum's period rooms, from Biedermeier and Regency on, should omit the characteristic keyboard instruments, readapted from generation to generation to the prevailing furniture style.

There is a fascinating variety of shape and decoration in eighteenth and nineteenth century pianos. The square piano (called a *Tafelklavier* in Germany), such as the Museum's Zumpe piano (22), was very popular and considerably cheaper to manufacture than the wing-shaped instruments (*Flügel*). Like the harpsichord in earlier centuries, the piano developed an upright version, of which the lyre and giraffe pianos (see 25) became typical appointments of the fashionable Biedermeier interior and its French and English counterparts, the Louis Philippe and Regency styles.

Of Chopin's and Liszt's time the Museum possesses a beautiful instrument made around 1830 in London by the famous firm of Erard (26), which is important not only as a step in the technical development of the piano, but outstanding also in its lavish intarsia decoration done by George Henry Blake. The founder of the firm, Sébastien Erard (1752-1832), was the ingenious inventor of the double escapement, which is now an indispensable part of the modern pianoforte. Another piano (27), made about 1850 by the firm of Nunns and Clark of New York to be exhibited at the Crystal Palace Exhibition of 1851, is the last word in Victorian ostentation. It may be a horror to devotees of functional beauty, yet it is as representative, as stylistic extreme, of its time as is the gilded harpsichord of the baroque.

25. Giraffe pianoforte, by Friedrich Voigt. German, early XIX *century. Lent by Miss Van Buren*

(opposite) Detail of the marquetry case of 26, designed and executed by George Henry Blake

26. Pianoforte, by Erard. English (London), about 1830. Gift of Mrs. Henry McSweeney, 1959

27. *Pianoforte, by Nunns and Clark. American (New York), about 1850.*
Gift of George Lowther, 1906